Bury St. Edmunds
in old picture postcards

by Mary S. Basham

European Library ZALTBOMMEL / THE NETHERLANDS

BACK IN TIME

GB ISBN 90 288 1350 0

© 1999 European Library – Zaltbommel/The Netherlands

Introduction

Bury St. Edmunds: Shrine of a King, Cradle of the Law

It is debatable whether, without Bury St. Edmunds, there would ever have been a Magna Carta and subsequently the basis of the American Constitution and a number of other important 'bills of right', including Amnesty International's high ideals. Why is this so? Because it was ostensibly as pilgrims to the great Abbey of St. Edmund, named after the martyred Saxon king, that twenty-five of England's mighty barons were able to meet in secret on 20 November 1214 and declare that they would force King John to observe rule of law – Magna Carta.

To walk the streets of the town centre today, is to walk the same routes and see the same squares those barons and the many thousands of other pilgrims to the shrine of St. Edmund would have known. Laid out on a grid pattern system by Abbot Baldwin, one of the first town planners, Bury St. Edmunds still has its Square for God (Angel Hill) and Square for the People (Cornhill), together with the magnificent Abbey Gate, Norman Tower, Cathedral Church of St. James and impressive parish church of St. Mary's. Add the ruins of the Abbey, the lazy flowing River Lark running through the formally laid out Abbey Gardens and entry roads to the town bearing their old 'gate' names, such as Northgate, Southgate and Risbygate, and you have a time capsule worth protecting from the ever present threat of modernity.

The only way to fully understand the development of Bury St. Edmunds from its early religious origins, through its days of medieval monastic might, and later, following the Dissolution, the years that brought seventeenth century confusion, Georgian grandeur and Victorian trade, is to explore the town for yourself. Look at the lines of old houses, the wealth of styles, the fine features that make up an ancient place. Investigate what the archives and museums have to offer, but above all else, talk to born and bred Burians who will only be too delighted to tell you about their town.

Acknowledgements

It is still difficult for me to think of St. Edmundsbury Borough Council as incorporating so much more than the town itself, or that West Suffolk no longer exists but has become simply Suffolk. Apart from these minor adjustments to my mental picture, I have been extremely fortunate to have lived, and later worked, in the town during a time when colourful characters were valued and living memory had so much to offer.

I would like to thank the many people who contributed to my columns during my days at the Bury Free Press and its sister papers and to all those who were willingly interviewed for my 'Look Back at Anglia' series on the former Saxon Radio, now part of SGR. Their help was invaluable in recording the past, and wherever possible I have tried to place material with the Suffolk Records Office for others to use in the future.

Finally I would like to dedicate this book to Theo Cutting, my mentor and friend, who in the days of blue pencil editing, welded it on my work with the alacrity of an Iceni warrior scything through a field of Romans. Thank you Theo.

1 There has been a twice-weekly market at Bury St. Edmunds since the Middle Ages, when it sprawled over the Cornhill and the Buttermarket in much the same way as it does today, or as this picture shows, in the early years of this century. It is still possible to stand on the pavement by the Post Office and see a similar scene, with Moyses Hall and its clock keeping an attentive eye on brisk trading. There are plenty of customers for locally grown fruit and vegetables, fresh fish from the coast, delicious cheeses, household goods, height of fashion garments or a snazzy hat to brighten up the day.

Market Hill, showing Moyses' Hall

Bury St. Edmunds

2　On very few occasions has the weather ever prevented a market being held in the town on a Wednesday and Saturday. Even the great winter storms of 1948 failed to halt the hardiest traders from turning up and plying their wares. Little wonder then that this snowy market day in the early 1900s still saw stalls lining the Buttermarket and warmly-clad shoppers out to make their purchases. Chapman's, established 1829, merchant tailor, outfitter, hatter and hosier, seen on the right, later became Smart and Farries, outfitters, suppliers of both working and best clothes for gentlemen. The property now houses a nationally-known company selling cosmetics and toiletries, but externally remains largely unchanged..

3 When this photograph was taken the area was known locally as Haken's Corner for obvious reasons. The shop, pictured centre, appears to have sold a wide variety of goods from glass and china to mops, brooms and galvanised buckets. By the 1930s the premises had changed trade to become the International Tea Company's Stores Ltd., and many will remember it as their favourite grocery shop before the advent of the supermarket. Next door on the left can be seen, George W. Wilson, watchmaker and jeweller, another familiar name. Countless young ladies will have spent time day-dreaming about engagement rings while looking in Wilson's windows!

4 When it came to choosing a site for a war memorial to commemorate West Suffolk soldiers killed in the South African campaign, the Cornhill was the obvious choice. Money was raised by public donation and the monument's unveiling took place on 11 November 1904 in the presence of townspeople sprinkled with dignitaries and local gentry. The ceremony was carried out by the commanding officer of troops in the Eastern District, Lord Methuen, who was met off the 12.09 train and escorted through the streets to the Cornhill by a mounted troop of the Duke of York's Own Loyal Suffolk Hussars. His stirring speech that day about keeping the country free from war in the future was to have a hollow ring within a decade.

5   An early view of the Cornhill looking north towards the Post Office. Ransomes, Sims & Jefferies Ltd., agricultural implement manufacturers, are clearly marked on the left, with Harwicke's drug store sandwiched in between by Felton's drapery shop. Further along, premises were occupied by O. P. Nice & Son, grocers, and Hunter & Oliver Ltd., wine merchants. The town's library was located in the building on the right, which also housed the Cullum Reference Library and collection of paintings. The Cullum family had formerly lived at Harwick House on the outskirts of Bury St. Edmunds and were very much regarded as local gentry.

Cornhill

Bury St. Edmunds

6 Built in 1771, the Market Cross (formerly the Town Hall) prominently featured above, was designed by Robert Adam as a playhouse. Believed to be his only public building in the Eastern region, it has served several purposes over the years, but is currently adapted for commercial use on the ground floor, while the upper floor is an art gallery. As a Grade I-listed building it has fortunately remained unaltered externally and lends a certain solid grace to the Cornhill panorama. This picture was taken around 1910, when, judging from the way everyone is looking towards the camera, photography was still a novelty.

7   Abbeygate Street is another of Bury St. Edmunds main shopping streets. Old and new properties line its length, with many of those shown in this picture still in existence today. The gabled shop on the left was Oliver & Son Ltd., provision merchants, who together with Thomas Ridley, further down the street, was considered the best in town. Although this photograph was taken before the Second World War, both businesses were still in existence during the years of post-war rationing. Local people of a 'certain age' may well remember sugar being weighed up into blue bags, butter cut from huge blocks shipped in from Australia, and sides of smoked bacon hanging from the rafters.

ABBEYGATE ST, BURY ST EDMUNDS.

8 The Fox Inn, Eastgate Street, looking very different in the early part of this century to its present plastered and painted façade. On the left, clinging onto the side of the road, is the Old Corner Shop, a casualty of the 1920s when it was demolished in favour of a row of houses. This part of Eastgate Street has always been prone to flooding and many people will be able to recall houses on the adjacent Broadway under water. In this photograph, however, it is the state of the road that is likely to pose a problem. Obviously most horse-power at the time came on four legs!

9 Taken from the top of the Norman Tower, this view across the rooftops will highlight lots of landmarks to the keen of eye. In the immediate foreground is the sloping roof of the Cathedral and the odd angles of the Athenaeum. The open space in front is the Angel Hill with no vehicles, either horse-drawn or horse-powered, in sight. Note also that the Angel Hotel is without any sign of its famous cloak of Virginia Creeper. It is also possible to make out Cupola House, the tiny steeple on top of Moyses Hall and in the distance, the tall spire of St. John's Church. If a similar photograph was taken today, it would still be possible to see the same points of reference.

Bury St. Edmunds from Norman Tower

10   Close-up of the Angel Hill taken in the 1920s. By now the Angel Hotel, pictured left, has acquired a covering of Virginia Creeper, but is otherwise largely unchanged from Victorian times when Charles Dickens was among its well-known patrons. It is thought the great man used the Angel as a setting for Pickwick Papers. Next door to the hotel is Pamela's, costumier, gowns, hatter and furrier, a favourite haunt of 'County' ladies looking for a special outfit. A much older property stands on the site of the present-day Borough Offices, while Angel Corner, an elegant Queen Anne house, graces the northern corner much as it does today. During the 40s and 50s mothers made a weekly trip to Angel Corner to collect baby milk powder, thick orange juice and jars of marmite to keep their offspring healthy.

Angel Hill, Bury St. Edmunds.

11   Eighty-six feet high and 36 feet wide, the Norman Tower was built in the first half of the twelfth century as a gateway to the Great Abbey church. Pilgrims would gather at the far end of Churchgate Street and process towards the huge tower's gaping door, through which it is said, you could see in the distance, a flame flickering on the Abbey's High Alter.

On the right of the picture is St. James' Cathedral Church, centre of the St. Edmundsbury diocese. Considerably restored by Sir Gilbert Scott in Victorian times, it has been sympathetically extended in recent years, with yet more additions to come.

Norman Tower and St. James' Church, Bury St. Edmunds.

12 You would have to look very carefully to identify this view today. Formerly part of the Great Abbey Church, it is known as the West Front and although technically a ruin, was converted into several dwellings sometime around the eighteenth century. These in turn, have been restored and modernised within the last few years with the help of English Heritage, to provide highly desirable residences. The many tombstones in this picture have been removed, the area grassed and left open plan to offset a rather fine statue of St. Edmund by Dame Elizabeth Frink. It was commissioned by West Suffolk County Council to mark the end of its independent status in 1974 on the formation of a united Suffolk County Council..

Bury St. Edmund's Abbey Ruins

13   The Great Churchyard viewed from in front of the Norman Tower. Although this photograph was taken around 1910 it still looks very much the same, with its avenue of trees, ancient tombstones and memorial to Protestants martyred in the reign of Mary I. Remains of the Chapel of the Charnel lie half-way down the avenue to the left. It contains a number of interesting plaques commemorating some of the town's famous or notorious former inhabitants including Henry Cockton, a Victorian novelist who numbered 'Valentine Vox the Ventriloquist' among his best-sellers. The Great Churchyard ceased to be the town's burial ground in the 1850s when a new cemetery was provided at the top of King's Road.

Martyrs' Memorial and Avenue, Bury St. Edmund

14   Originally, Bury St. Edmunds' beautifully kept Abbey Gardens were privately owned and maintained in the great Victorian tradition of a collection of botanical specimens. Only invited guests, and later membership, entitled anyone to walk among the intriguing and sometimes rare plants that had been brought back from the far flung corners of the earth. When this postcard was sent in 1910, it had just become possible for the general public to pay the botanical gardens a visit. The sender wrote that 'it would do Ted good to be here', implying that it was a tranquil place to spend a few hours. Thousands of visitors over the years would echo that!

Botanical Gardens, Bury St. Edmunds

15 What a difference a decade makes! Taken in the 1920s, this view of the Abbey Gardens, then known simply as The Park, reveals the extent of re-vamping the former botanical gardens had received. Gone the tangle of riotous growth, to be replaced by neatly clipped lawns, a few isolated yucca plants and the beginnings of the formal flower beds so evident today. Only the Abbey Gate remains unchanged and aloof, as if suspended in time. It was destroyed by the townspeople in the early fourteenth century following a revolt against monastic rule. However, they were forced to rebuild it at their own expense and the impressive result has endured since 1347, earning it a Grade I-listing.

The Park, Bury St. Edmunds.

16 Literally thousands of pupils took the route through the Abbey Gardens, across the bridge spanning the River Lark and up the hill to the King Edward VI Grammar School. Established by Royal Charter in 1550, the boys from KEGs in their black blazers with distinctive Tudor rose badge, were considered privileged to attend the famous school. This photograph is thought to have been taken in the 1930s, long before the building of the residential home that now occupies the river bank, or the Vinefields housing development. The school offered places not only to boys from the town but to bright scholars throughout West Suffolk. Some were borders, others 'day boys', all had to attend lessons five-and-a-half days a week.

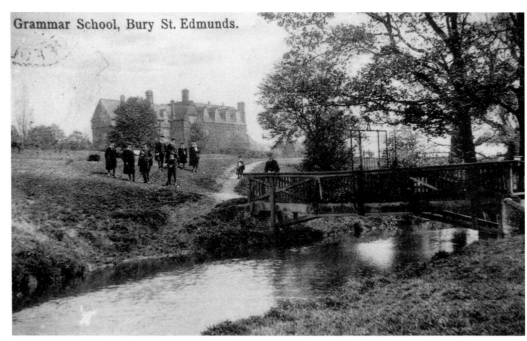

Grammar School, Bury St. Edmunds.

17   Probably taken in the 1930s, this view of Chequer Square is instantly recognisable. Dwarfed by the Norman Tower, the Tudor-style house on the right was erected in 1846 at a cost of £2,300 as a Penny Bank. It had almost 3,000 depositors in its hey-day but lost out when the Post Office Savings Bank opened. The square's earliest recording is on monastic maps as Paddokpool, a grassy space bordered on the north and east sides with trees. By 1748 it is marked up as Chequer Square and we can only assume that at sometime between the Dissolution of the monastery and the Georgian era, the government's revenue accounting house was situated nearby, hence the name change.

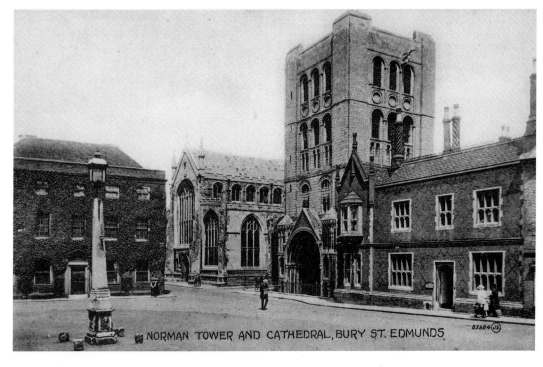

NORMAN TOWER AND CATHEDRAL, BURY ST. EDMUNDS.

18 Another instantly recognisable scene, for although the horse and trap, perambulators and style of dress place the date in the early part of this century, the buildings remain largely unchanged. On the right is the Guildhall, with its thirteenth century porch. It was regularly used as the Council Chamber from its foundation until 1966. On the left is a range of properties exhibiting mainly Georgian façades, but hiding much older features underneath. As now, they have long provided suitable addresses for solicitors and physicians. Many townspeople will remember Dr. Bromley at No. 81, and a little further down the street, Drs. Batt and Cory at No. 85.

GUILDHALL, BURY ST. EDMUNDS. 607

19 What a range of grocery stores shoppers on the Cornhill had to choose from in the 1920s. Not for them supermarkets and out of town shopping malls, this was an age when fresh food meant buying on the day. In this picture alone it is possible to pick out Lipton's, the Maypole, Home and Colonial Stores and the International Tea Co. The large blind and roof board on the right advertises Smith's Home Furnishing Stores, a company that many will remember trading well into the post-war years. It is interesting to note that obviously at the time this picture was taken no one considered themselves properly dressed without a hat. The men are in boaters, trilby's or flat caps, while the ladies seem to favour straw adorned with ribbons or flowers.

20 What has a sign of a Highlander got to do with Bury St. Edmunds? The answer is, it hung for many years in the entrance to Sexton's, tobacconist, at 26 Buttermarket and is now part of a local history display in Moyses Hall Museum. The story goes that the character was first used by a David Wishart of Coventry Street, London, before 1720, who, in addition to selling snuff, is rumoured to have owned a coffee house used by Jacobite sympathisers. After the Bonnie Prince Charlie uprising and defeat, Highland dress was banned for sometime, but the figure of the Highlander to advertise snuff – and hence tobacco – had become a firmly established sign by then.

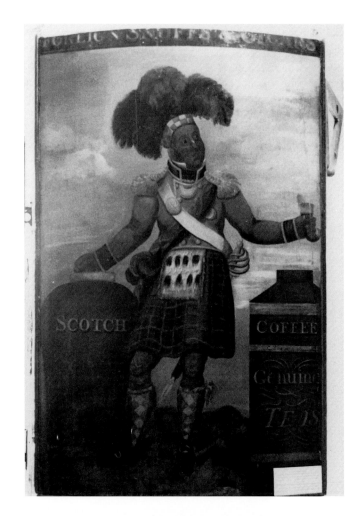

21 There are parts of the town where you can easily believe that nothing has changed in almost a century. One such spot is looking towards St. John's Church from the corner of Well Street where it joins Orchard Street. Neat, bay-fronted Victorian terraced houses line the road as they do in this photograph, taken before the First World War. The railings have largely disappeared though, they went to help the war effort, but otherwise a time traveller would feel at home. St. John's, consecrated in 1841 at a time of expansion in this part of Bury St. Edmunds, continues to reach up towards heaven, its spire piercing the town's skyline and visible for miles around.

St. John's Church, Bury St. Edmunds

22　This photograph shows Gibraltar Barracks, Out Risbygate, viewed from Westley Road. It was taken in the 1930s, when Major Pereira was the Commanding Officer. Apart from being the Suffolk Regiment's depot, it was also the base for the Suffolk Regiment Old Comrades' Association and the National Association for the Employment of Regular Sailors, Soldiers and Airmen (East Anglian Branch). It is a sobering thought to think how many young men signed up there and gave their lives for their country. Although the Keep remains and at present houses the regimental museum, the range of buildings in the background that once surrounded the Parade Ground, have been demolished. The Suffolk Regiment ceased to exist as the county's regiment in 1959, when it was amalgamated into what has since become the Royal Anglians.

THE BARRACKS, BURY ST. EDMUNDS. (23)　　　223/31.J.V.

23   Built in red-brick and designed in Free-Renaissance style by Frederick Barnes of Ipswich in 1846, Bury St. Edmunds' Railway Station is one of its many surviving gems. When this picture was taken it was known as Northgate Station, as, in the early days of the 'iron horse', there was another station in Eastgate Street. The train brought a real sense of freedom for ordinary folk. Suddenly it was possible to travel to the seaside, the races or even London – there and back in a day. Once a line was established through to Newmarket in the west and Ipswich in the east, anything seemed possible. The Eastgate Station serviced a track to Long Melford, easing transport for travellers who would otherwise have had to make the journey towards the Essex border by carrier's cart.

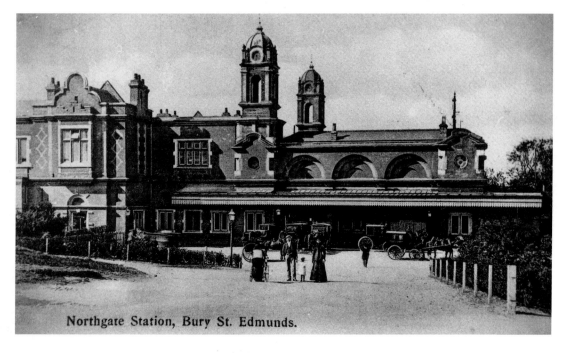

Northgate Station, Bury St. Edmunds.

24 A visit 'up the hospital' today for people from Bury St. Edmunds or the surrounding district means just that, heading up a slight rise to the former Hardwick Heath, site of the West Suffolk General Hospital since the 1970s. For a 150 years before that, the hospital had been located 'near Westgate – on land known as Barrow Close, with lime kilns to the front and rear'. The small road leading to it, formerly Chevington Road, was later more aptly named Hospital Road. Patients admitted in the very early days were required to bring clean clothing and a change of linen. Impeccable behaviour was expected, no smoking, drinking, gambling or swearing, and certainly no complaints. Taken around 1905, this photograph says it all. Just look at the shine on the floor!

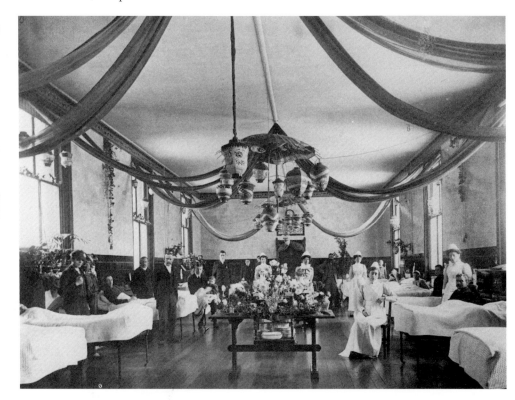

25 Looking up the Butter-market from Abbeygate Street, this view was taken in 1907 to celebrate the opening of the first great pageant depicting the history of Bury St. Edmunds. It looks as if most of the town turned out to watch the procession go by. The Suffolk Hotel was already in existence and opposite, with the attractive windows, boots and shoes were sold by Fox and Mawe. The shop later became W.H. Cullen and Son, clothiers, with the Cullen family residing on the first floor and domestic help on the second. It is said the shop's cellar had several blocked-up doorways and like many such properties in the town, these doorways supposedly led to tunnels connecting through to the abbey.

26   Less than a decade later, the Buttermarket looked very different on the morning of 30 April 1915 following the first Zeppelin raid over the town. Lit by a full moon, Bury St. Edmunds was an easy target for more than fifty incendiary bombs, one of which penetrated the roof of Day's, bootmaker at 32 Buttermarket. The shop was soon engulfed by flames that quickly spread to adjacent properties used by Mrs. Ellen Wise, a ladies' outfitter; T.H. Nice & Company, motor and cycle agents; Miss Alice Clark, tobacconist; Johnson Brothers Ltd., dyers; and George Cousins, photographer. The latter took the opportunity to capture some spectacular pictures! Although in danger, the Suffolk Hotel was saved by the Fire Brigade's preventative action. Not quite a year later the town suffered a further raid, although this time the centre was not a target.

27 Bury St. Edmunds could boast three cinemas – the Odeon, Central and Playhouse – during the decades when going to the 'pictures' was considered the highlight of the week. It is the Playhouse that features in the foreground of this 1930s photograph of the Buttermarket. More than just a cinema, it doubled as a theatre, especially in the 1950s when many will remember going there for Christmas pantomimes and shows like the 'Desert Song'. The Half Moon bar, part of the Playhouse complex, also figured strongly in a good night out, providing an early evening rendezvous or an ideal place for meeting up with friends later.

BUTTER MARKET, BURY ST. EDMUNDS

28 This is a view of the Cornhill taken in the 1930s. Smiths Furnishing Company is still the most prominent name, with the International Stores occupying the corner site. Soon after this picture was taken the shop with the blind became the Chain Library, a source of endless pleasure for avid readers, especially ladies who loved nothing better than a good romance. It cost a few pence to borrow a book, but it was money well spent. Woods, leather goods outlet, next door, later became Lawson's, wireless engineers. The company was founded by Cyril Lawson, whose original trade was repairing and rebuilding motorcycles. A keen motorcycle racing enthusiast and inventor, he brought the first television pictures to the town.

CORN HILL, BURY ST. EDMUNDS

29 The 1950s and the Cornhill had its own traffic congestion problems. Alongside Woolworth's on the right of the picture, G.W. Henshall at 25 and 26 supplied both trade and retail customers with everything from nuts and bolts to bathroom fittings. The distinctive lock trademark hung from the upper floor rather like an inn sign, very much in keeping with the traditional method of advertising wares in the days of the Guilds. Next door, Annette's dress shop stocked special occasion garments and high class gowns. To walk through the door of Annette's with a wedding in mind was to walk into a world where dreams could come true.

Cornhill, Bury St. Edmunds

30   If you stand outside 11 Guildhall Street and catch the light in the right direction you can still glimpse a fragment of the past. Etched into the top of the window is C.C. Pudney & Co., who were electrical engineers throughout the first half of the century. Much of the domestic electricity in and around the town was the work of the company and some of those who trained with the firm went on to join the Eastern Electricity Board after its post-war formation. Pictured left to right in this photograph are electrician George Pilfold, storeman George Bridges, who later worked for the GPO, and Ernie De Main, a Guildhall Street resident.

31 Town centre public houses and inns have always been great meeting places on market days, especially Wednesdays, when the Livestock Market attracts farmers and stockmen from miles around. In the days before animals were brought in by transport, they would be herded in through Bury St. Edmunds' busy streets and the proverbial 'bull in a china shop' often had real meaning then. After such excitement, the hospitality of the Three Kings Hotel adjacent to Market Thoroughfare was a welcome retreat. Pictured in the late 1930s when the host was Joseph Bernstein, the Three Kings had a reputation for substantial steak and kidney pies, strong ale and masculine ambience.

32   The East Anglian Electric Supply Company sited its first power station off Prospect Row and the Playfields. It was a simple construction that produced energy by converting rubbish into heat. The heat in turn boiled water to drive turbines and enough electricity resulted from what was fondly called the 'dust destructor', to light the town and power a hooter that heralded two minutes silence on Armistice Sunday. In August 1943 explosions at the station caused many people to believe the enemy had arrived. Years later it emerged a limpet device had been attached to a condenser at the back of the building, supposedly by a double agent who had been instructed to 'blow up a food storage depot in London, an ammunitions store in Hampshire and part of the power station in Bury St. Edmunds.

33   At 96 Risbygate Street, Wells, corn, seed and agricultural merchants supplied the needs of local farmers. Here they bought their wellington boots, milking coats, pails and pitchers, spring seed and cattle feed to see them through the winter. Domestic pets requirements were met by a second outlet in Short Brackland and many people may remember that two monkeys occupied a cage just inside the door. A better pair of pick-pockets would have been hard to find and when their skill became too finely tuned to excuse any longer, they were donated to the Abbey Gardens as apart of an animal menagerie.

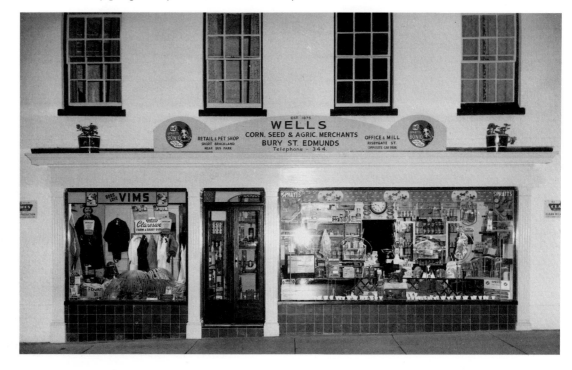

34   Marlow & Co, timber and builders merchants, were a familiar part of the College Street scene. Originally the company had a timber yard at 12a, adjoining Barnaby's Almshouses, but eventually these properties were also taken over by the firm, as this picture shows. One of the oldest streets in the town, College Street began its existence as Hennescotestrete, lying opposite Hethenmannestrete – now Hatter Street. It was sparsely populated until the building of the College of Jesus, a hostel for secular clergy around the late fifteenth century, when the name change was almost certainly instigated.

In more recent history College Street will be remembered by numerous children attending the Guildhall Feoffment School, a mixed junior establishment.

35 One of Marlow's delivery vehicles pictured in the early 1930s. The timber yard supplied both trade and individual customers and was a Mecca for anything to do with wood – and later, when the firm expanded, all types of building supplies. The yard lay at the back of College Street, with a showroom outlet and additional entrance on Churchgate Street. The company also at one time owned land on the other side of College Street, adjoining College Lane, and a range of gabled houses that had formerly been part of the old workhouse. The firm is still trading in the town, although from a much larger site in Hollow Road, and now includes a garden centre.

36 Swept away in a huge demolition programme during recent years, this part of Westgate Street was often referred to by local residents as Hellfire Corner. Exactly why it should have acquired that name is lost in the mists of time, although some think it may have been in reference to the volume of traffic that took the corner with great difficulty. As the name appears to go back further than the days of horsepower, this seems unlikely. In living memory the shop on the corner housed greengrocers Fursland & Maltby, with a barber's at No. 33 and next door a sweet shop, which was a favourite with children making their way to St. Peter's Infants School in Hospital Road.

37 The name Boby has been associated with business in Bury St. Edmunds since 1843, when Robert Boby established an ironmonger's shop at 7, Meat Market, now Cornhill. The business grew to manufacture 'improvements in corn dressing and winnowing machines', and these in turn earned many accolades and sales at home and abroad. In 1861 additional space was acquired in St. Andrew's Street South and a large machine shop was built, trading under the name Robert Boby Ltd. During the First World War the company was given contracts to manufacture armaments, but following the Armistice, returned to the making of agricultural and malting equipment. Many local young men did their engineering apprenticeships with the company, whose influence on Bury St. Edmunds can still be seen in street names and foundation stones. The picture above was taken earlier this century and features workers who manned one of the huge boilers at the plant.

38   For many years Bury St. Edmunds has taken a keen pride in its floral displays and 'Bury in Bloom' has become a regular feature of the town's summer season. However, the Abbey Gardens remain the real show piece, with the formal flower beds set out in intricate designs and a multitude of colours. The process of turning the once botanical gardens into its present highly structure format has evolved over many decades and required a labour of love from a continual turnover of dedicated gardeners. The picture shows the north wall area being cleared earlier this century, when it was customary for gardeners to wear a collar and tie for work and be supervised by a uniformed park-keeper.

39 Working Men's Clubs, Smoking Clubs, the Constitutional Club, Bury St. Edmunds has never been short of places for men to meet on social ground – and in some instances, from a young age. One such was the Cycling Club, founded almost as soon as the bicycle was invented and still going strong in a different form today. Pictured are members of the club out for the day in the very early years of this century, when owning a bicycle was a luxury few could afford. Obviously, even though your legs might not be long enough to reach the pedals, it was highly desirable to be photographed perched on the saddle, as the young man on the right demonstrates.

40 The part Bury St. Edmunds played in the formation of the Magna Carte has made certain of the town's place in history. However, long before the Barons met at the Abbey's High Altar to discuss the great document, Beodricksworth, as it was once known, was a name to be reckoned with, and as such, has provided rich grounds for researchers. In this century alone two 'epic' pageants have portrayed the life and times of the area from the years of Roman occupation to Charles Dickens days, when the Angel Hotel provided a backdrop for his storytelling. The photograph on this and the three following pages are all scenes and characters from the first pageant that was staged in the Edwardian era. Here, Boadicea is pictured gathering her Iceni tribe before leading a revolt against the Romans.

41　In this scene the young Saxon King Edmund, who had ruled over East Anglia for a decade, meets Lothbroc, leader of the invading Danish forces, and makes him welcome at his Court in the belief that you must 'love thine enemies'. Unfortunately, one of Edmund's followers murders Lothbroc. The Danes blame Edmund and ultimately put him to death by tying him to a tree, shooting him through with arrows and decapitating him. It is the legend surrounding the King's death that forms the basis of Bury St. Edmunds' insignia, a wolf guarding Edmund's head. After the establishment of the Abbey in the town, the young King's remains were allegedly buried in the Great Church and became a focus for pilgrimages.

42 Bury St. Edmunds has never lacked royal visitors and the scriptwriters for the two great pageants have had a field day portraying one particular visit, that of Henry VI and Queen Margaret. The royal pair and their Court came to the town in 1447 when Parliament was summoned to sit in the Abbey's refectory. The occasion was the trial of Humphrey, Duke of Gloucester, on grounds of high treason. Many stories have been penned about this event and the subsequent death of the Duke, who was found dead in his bed at the Hostel of St. Saviours before the trial could get underway. Doubtless, many more theories will be committed to paper in centuries to come as mystery and speculation continues to intrigue historians!

43   People from all walks of life were recruited to take part in the pageant and while the starring roles went to talented would-be actors and actresses, numerous others were lined up to play extras. Boadicea's Iceni tribe alone accounted for fifty people, whose only requirements were that they could look convincing and come up with their own costumes. Harry Double, pictured, then in his 40s and working for a local building company, jumped at the chance to take part, bringing along a Zulu spear as a authentic looking prop. Who knows where he got the wig from? And would an Iceni, circa 60 AD, have been clean shaven except for a moustache?

44 Hardwick, on the outskirts of Bury St. Edmunds, was always a great favourite with local people as a place to walk and court. It was also well-known as the annual venue for a huge fete. In post-war years this meant a famous singer or personality like Sabrina helping to raise money for charity, but originally the occasion was the Temperance Fete. This picture, taken in August 1910, demonstrates just how popular the fete was. Literally hundreds made the long walk from the town to the Hardwick grounds. Dressed in their best, everyone with a hat, even the small children, the Temperance Fete was a day to anticipate and enjoy, with relish.

45 What had the crowd at the Temperance Fete in August 1910 come to see? The amazing, daring and altogether spectacular A.E. Henley and his Company! At a time when any sort of entertainment was usually home-grown, a troupe of professional acrobats, trick cyclists, clowns, singers and dancers promised excitement unlimited. Souvenir copies of the Company's photograph were eagerly sought, much as pop stars pictures are today. The proud owner of this one, a small child at the time of purchase, remembers she thought the lady singer, seated second from the right, was the most glamorous person she had ever seen.

46 The end of the First World War could not have been more welcome than in Bury St. Edmunds. The region had lost thousands of young men to the conflict, its county regiments having taken an active part in many of the toughest battles, like the Somme. Those that had not died on the battlefield came home to either die of gas poisoning or bear the scars of shell shock for many years to come. In this photograph it is time for the town to celebrate peace at last. A wreath hanging from the Abbey Gate proclaims 'Great Britain'. The banners and flags are out, the Cathedral choir is assembled, Aldermen and Mayor in place, attended by the Mace Bearers. It is time for the band (right) to rouse the crowd with regimental music.

47 Like most ancient towns and boroughs, Bury St. Edmunds owns some fine pieces of ceremonial insignia. Pictured here are the two Sergeants-at-Mace, or Mace Bearers, and the Sword Bearer, whose job it was to precede the Mayor and Council on civic occasions. The maces were commissioned in the seventeenth century at a grand cost of £54 each. The sword was a gift to the Borough by Sir John Hervey. It is thought the photograph was taken in the 1920s and that the gentleman on the right is John (Jack) Pilfold, who for many years was foreman for the Council. On his retirement he took up the part-time post of Market Inspector, keeping order among the stallholders on Wednesdays and Saturdays.

48 Officers and Sergeants of the Volunteer Training Corps 2nd Battalion Suffolk Regiment 'A' Company are pictured in the town at the end of the First World War. The equivalent of the Territorial Army today, it was customary for most established regiments to have a volunteer force. The 'Suffolks' date back to 1685 and were originally formed by the 7th Duke of Norfolk to meet James II's perceived threat from the Monmouth Rebellion. During its long history the regiment gained numerous battle honours, including Minden and the Siege of Gibraltar. A castle and key, with the motto 'Montis In-signia Calpe' became the regimental crest, Calpe being the ancient name for Gibraltar. The 'Suffolks' joined with the county regiments of Norfolk and Cambridgeshire in 1959 to constitute part of the East Anglian Regiment, that in turn has become the Royal Anglians.

49   The Cornhill on market day pictured in the 1920s. The view is taken looking towards the International Stores on the corner, and on the left down St. John's Street. In those days the market was obviously not as strictly laid out as it today. Stalls seem to be placed higgledy-piggledy. The Market Inspector's hut is in the foreground on the left and it was his duty to enforce standards and collect the market toll from each trader. Traffic does not appear to have been a problem at this stage, unlike now when the Cornhill area is closed to vehicles until 4 p.m. Barrows were simply gathered together in some confusion and left until required, as in the foreground.

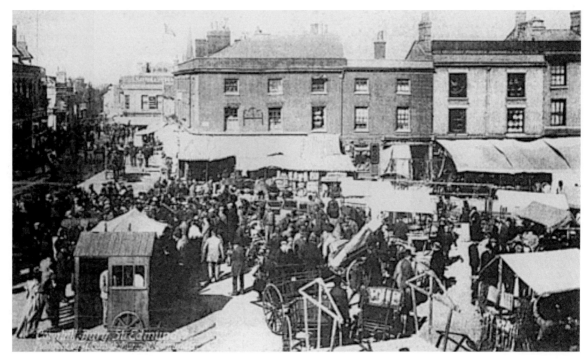

50   Like any small town pre-1950s, Bury St. Edmunds was made up of long standing families, many of them with ties stretching back centuries. Parish registers, such as those of St. Mary's, record births, deaths and marriages with familiar surnames, making tracing family trees both revealing and complex. The Hagger family was typical of the time, generation upon generation being born and bred locally. This picture, taken at the family home in Church Row early on this century, shows three generations, the newest addition wearing the traditional christening robe. It was customary in Suffolk for a silver coin to be sewn in the hem for each baby who wore it. The christening shawl too was very special and the best were those made so fine they could be drawn through a mother's wedding ring.

51 Opened in 1922 by the Mayor, Councillor J. Parkington, Bury St. Edmunds own swimming pool was a novelty few young men – or women – could resist. The water was never very warm, a top temperature of around 60°F being considered a luxury, but the pool offered a grand opportunity to impress. It was a different tale though for those using the adjoining baths. Water for a nice hot, private soak was heated by the nearby power station and provided a much appreciated weekly treat for those without a bathroom at home or the opportunity to use a bungalow bath beside a fire.

52 Although the new swimming pool was a much needed facility for the town, a privileged few of Bury St. Edmunds' residents had been able to use two other local pools. As early as 1870, William Lot Jackman, a mason and builder of some note, constructed a covered pool on the corner of Westgate Street and Maynewater Lane and laid a commemorative stone, as shown. The pool was not very big and we shall never know why he built it in the first place, but in 1893 it was taken over by the Council and eventually ended up as a private facility for employees of Greene King brewery. An open-air pool was also built for staff working at the Hand Laundry off Hardwick Lane. It was seen as a welcome means of cooling off after the heat and steam generated by the laundry's boilers.

53 No. 58 College Street was the headquarters of Bury St. Edmunds' Boy Scouts. It was here that numerous young lads proudly learnt to tie knots, kindle a fire without matches and cook a nourishing meal in a tin can. The date of this photograph is not certain but it is thought to be either just before or just after the Second World War. What it does demonstrate is that uniformity in both dress and style was desirable. The Scouts turned out to walk in parades, they were there to join the May Queen's procession and to take their place in church at Christmas. The headquarters of the sister organisations, the Girl Guides and Brownies, was at St. Mary's House, Whiting Street.

54 Eastgate Street was always regarded as a self contained community. Even in the 1950s families never moved far away from the 'Street' and when they got married frequently found a house or rooms to rent within a stone's throw of their parents. This picture is typical and illustrates the closeness of the area and the important part the local shop played in day-to-day life. It was taken outside Mr. Taylor's shop. He is the man without a jacket, fourth from the left. Among those also present are Mr. Plampin and Mr. Boggis, both long standing family names connected with Eastgate Street.

55 Taken at the end of a very successful year, 1945-1946, this picture of the Bury Town Football Club reveals the strength of support the team had from its board and older players.

It was a hands-on association, with everyone helping out to get the ground ready for matches and to assist back at the clubhouse. When this photograph was taken, and for quite a while afterwards, the football ground was off King's Road on land adjoining the Playfields, now part of Parkway and the town carparks. There was a rather ancient wood and galvanised iron stand on the north side, otherwise devoted supporters were expected to brave the elements.

56 Canon Wintle, the 'Barrel Organ' man, was a familiar sight and sound on the streets of Bury St. Edmunds from the time he became rector of Lawshall in 1923 until his death in 1959. Born in London, he was brought up with the music of the 'tingle-tangles' that played near his home. When he became a young curate in Manchester, he attempted to learn the art of setting a tune from one of his parishioners. Eventually he mastered the technique more by trial and error and decided to put his hobby to good use by providing employment for out-of-work agricultural labourers during the Depression. He established a workshop in Lawshall to manufacture barrel organs and as each one was completed, sent it onto the streets with a minder to help raise money for the needy.

WITH BEST WISHES
FROM
A O wintle.
1955.

Lawshall Rectory,
Bury St. Edmunds.

57 Every barrel organ completed in Canon Wintle's workshop was personally stamped, as this picture shows. Minders were expected to be scrupulously honest and tales abound of the Canon's reaction to anyone who stopped off on the way home to quench their thirst out of the takings. Despite this somewhat awesome image he was much loved and in 1959 became more than a local character, when he began broadcasting on the BBC Home Service. Many people will remember his music brightening up the streets, especially at Christmas, when one of his favourite 'pitches' was the corner of Whiting Street and Abbeygate Street.

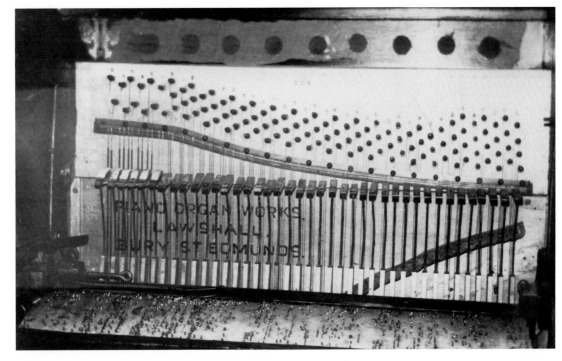

58 The Corn Exchange was the venue for the Annual Horticultural Show. This was the event of the year for keen gardeners from the town and surrounding district. It is believed this picture was taken during the early 1950s and shows the Mayor making his leisurely perusal of the stands. Although dahlias and tomatoes feature prominently in this particular display, much competition centred on chrysanthemums in all their various shapes and colours. The gentleman, second from the right, Charles 'Jim' Meekins, was an expert in growing dwarf chrysanthemums and usually managed to win a cup or two for his entries.

59 For over three hundred years until 1966, the town's governing body met in the Guildhall. This picture is taken of a Council meeting in full swing. It shows the Mayor, presiding at the top of the table, and the Bury St. Edmunds' insignia of two maces and sword laid out to denote that the meeting is in session. The Guildhall itself is one of the town's oldest surviving buildings. It features a thirteenth century porch and additional chambers, including the banqueting chamber, a gift to the town by Jankyn Smyth, a fifteenth century benefactor. He was also responsible for funding the building of the chancel chapels in St. Mary's Church and a trust which benefits the poor.

60 On the next three pages are moments frozen in time that encapsulate the early post-war years. The picture, taken in the big room at the back of the Black Boy inn, Guildhall Street, typifies a children's Christmas party in what was still a period of austerity. The landlord had made sure there was a tree, but decorations were scarce. After fish paste sandwiches, jelly and blancmange, and a slice of cake, games were the highlight of the day, with prizes like a packet of Jelly Babies or a handkerchief. Not for these 'Baby Boomers' the luxury of today's designer frocks and labelled sweat shirts, but everyone was turned out in their Sunday best, even if it meant parents saving up clothing coupons for months in advance.

61 A few years on and senior school in Bury St. Edmunds meant the County Grammar in Northgate Street, the King Edward VI Grammar School for Boys off Eastgate Street, or the Silver Jubilee Schools in Grove Road. Although the latter shared a building, single sex education was provided, with boys attending one side and girls on the other. Both schools operated strictly according to traditional values under the direction of the headmaster, Mr. Pettit, and headmistress, Mrs. Crocker. The uniform was bottle green and as the picture shows, in summer gingham frocks were the order of the day for the young ladies.

62 At the other end of the spectrum, long service to one company was marked at various points along the way. In this picture George Pilfold, master electrician, is being presented with a gold watch for 25 years service to the Electricity Board. The presentation was made at the Board's Playfield premises and included many of his colleagues. This was still a time when the only way to learn a trade or craft was to serve an apprenticeship of up to seven years. During those years an apprentice earned very little as it was regarded as a privilege to be training alongside a master. Some masters were more patient and better teachers than others!

63   Booty is a name synonymous with Northgate Street since the 1930s. A family business in the true sense of the word, while the shop sold fruit, vegetables and general goods, John Booty, pictured here, delivered milk produced on the family's farm at Timworth. Deliveries were made by horse and cart, 'Sandy' providing the horsepower. On hot summer days, those who received their milk in the afternoon stood the risk of it arriving as cheese, for Sandy liked to take his time. He knew all the customers likely to offer a crust of bread or a juicy apple and nothing would shake him from his routine.

64 Another horse-drawn vehicle on the streets of Bury St. Edmunds was the Rag and Bone man. In this picture, Les Freeman, one of the best known in the town, is starting out to work his patch. The results of a day's effort would usually end up at Brahams in Risbygate Street. The firm dealt mainly in scrap metals like copper and lead, but it also took in all kinds of rags. These were sorted into quality and colour, their zips, hooks and eyes removed and buttons cut off before being sent for re-cycling. Furs were the top end of the range and eagerly sought for making into coats, hats and the backing on gloves. A rabbit's skin was worth 6d, a hare's 9d and as much as four shillings for an undamaged mole's.

65 Jack Mulley, another of the town's colourful characters, pictured beside one of his vehicles painted in the distinctive company colours of orange and cream. Born and bred in Ixworth, a small village just outside of Bury St. Edmunds, Jack Mulley began his love of all things motorised by working for a local garage. There he liked nothing better than a chance to polish the headlamps on the firm's omnibuses. In 1938 he took a gamble and bought up an unsuccessful garage, complete with buses, licenses and attendant problems for £150. The first trip he ever made under his own name was driving the Ixworth Football Club to Stradishall in a bus with the registration UT 7836. It was to be the first of many!

66 By the 1950s Mulley's Motorways had grown to a fleet of vehicles. Trips to the races at Newmarket or Great Yarmouth, a day's shopping in Norwich, excursion to the seaside or a Saturday afternoon home game at Ipswich were all part of the service offered by Jack Mulley's company. On one occasion 22 buses loaded with supporters left the Angel Hill in Bury St. Edmunds for a 'big match' at Norwich at a cost of three shillings per passenger return fare. Pictured are just some of the Mulley's fleet in a stately procession from the Cornhill. It says something about the era that, although the clock on the left indicates that it is almost noon, traffic is very light. It would not be the same today!

67 The inauguration of a new bus with a ribbon cutting ceremony outside The Castle Hotel on the Cornhill is the subject of this photograph. The Castle was a favourite spot for picking up passengers, for the hotel provided welcome shelter if the weather was wet and the bus late! Smith's furnishing company is still very much in evidence to the left, as is Lawson's electrical goods, next door. As a tailpiece to the story of Mulley's Motorways, Jack Mulley sold the firm on his retirement in the early 1980s, but the new owners had the wisdom to retain the company's famous colours.

68 With the outbreak of the Second World War Bury St. Edmunds was seen as a safe haven for children evacuated from cities like London. In the very first week of war being declared, trainloads of children began arriving at Northgate Street Station, each wearing a label bearing his or her name and age. Most had only a small suitcase full of belongings and for many it was their first glimpse of the countryside. This picture illustrates the trepidation the children must have felt in coming to a strange place to live with people they did not know.

69 Once out of the station and onto the forecourt, the evacuees were split up into groups and despatched to families who were willing to take them in. It was not an easy task, with something like three hundred children arriving with each special train and the 'sorting out' fell mainly to the Red Cross and to helpful local ladies. Transport was seconded from omnibus companies and firms such as Hunter and Oliver, wine merchants, who made a delivery van available. Most children remained in and around the town, but some were taken to nearby villages, where they found country life a complete mystery after living in places like the East End.

70 Despite the apparent rural position of Bury St. Edmunds, the town was surrounded by airfields during the Second World War and the drone of planes frequently filled the skies overhead. A Forces Centre was set up in a house on Chequer Square, where tea, sympathy and conversation could be found most afternoons. There was also a dire need to keep morale high and various types of entertainment were devised, including tea dances, revues, and as this photograph illustrates, concerts of great variety in the guise of wartime follies. Where else could you expect to find Gypsy Petulengro and Pattie sharing the same bill as Memories of Chu Chin Chow?

71   In 1948 a slim volume entitled 'Suffolk Summer' was published, the work of John Appleby, an American serviceman stationed here during the last months of the war. It has since been reprinted many times, for it perfectly encapsulates the time and tide of life visiting personnel found themselves experiencing far from their own homelands. Pictures like the one shown convey both glamour and bravado, but one cannot help wondering whether those smiling faces really felt as confident as they look. Some of the famous planes that droned off from local airfields and had the luck to return, are now part of the Imperial War Museum exhibits at Duxford near Cambridge.

72 Like everywhere throughout the country, Bury St. Edmunds was expected to turn out its own 'Dad's Army' and it did! Pictured are the Home Guard, around 1943, lined up for inspection on the Parade Ground of the Territorial Barracks in King's Road. Censorship would not allow the names of the officers to be mentioned in the local report that accompanied the picture at the time, but perhaps someone will be able to come up with the answer now. Apart from drilling at the barracks, the Home Guard were often taken on training exercises to Lackford Heath or to adjoining forestry land.

The Home Guard is Ready!

73 And then it was all over and Bury St. Edmunds went wild! These next two pictures are typical of what went on in every city, town and village throughout the country. The bunting and flags went up, banners made, precious tins of fruit donated, sandwiches spread with hoarded honey and from somewhere, someone managed to produce a cake, such was the ingenuity of people who had waited too long for peace to return. This photograph was taken in the Long Brackland, a community that had always known how to look after its own. Sad to think that within a few years much of the area would be swept away in a grand programme of modernisation.

74 Taken at the College Street party to celebrate the end of the war, this photograph illustrates that everyone felt they wanted a share of the fun. From somewhere mothers managed to make costumes, although occasionally what was lacking in material or skill had to be made up for with imagination. Coronation Day 1953 and the Queen's Silver Jubilee in 1977 have also brought out the street party instinct and produced their own versions of the Fancy Dress Competition. As for the adults of College Street and neighbouring Whiting Street, after the children were safely tucked up in bed, it was time for dancing the night away to the latest Big Band sound – so I am told!

75 The last two pictures appropriately both tell very 'final' stories. Here is the doorway of the old Jail in Southgate Street. It was from here that the last public hanging in the town took place on Monday, 11 August 1828, when William Corder of Polstead swung for the murder of Maria Marten in the notorious Red Barn case. Much has been written about the crime, plays performed, details gone over time and again and still the fascination continues. Yet every day thousands of motorists drive past the gateway without realising that this was the scene of such a famous execution, an execution that had those attending clamouring to buy an inch of the rope as a macabre souvenir!

76 'And finally' as they say, in the Charnel House within the Great Churchyard in Bury St. Edmunds, is a memorial stone to Henry Cockton, a much misunderstood man. A Londoner by birth, he married the daughter of the landlady who kept the Seven Stars inn, Long Brackland and quickly made a name for himself penning successful novels. Unfortunately, money and Henry did not go well together, nor did his ability to invest wisely for his mother-in-law, who when things went wrong, reaped her own form of revenge. Henry was only in his 40s when he died, a poor and broken man. He received no proper recognition of his literary achievements until the plaque was raised to his memory some thirty years after his death.